KNOTS AROUND THE HOME

A Practical Guide for Practical People

Bob Newman and Tami Knight

With illustrations by Tami Knight

Menasha
Ridge
Press

Library of Congress Cataloging-in-Publication Data

Newman, Bob, 1958-.
Knots around the home : a practical guide for practical people
    Bob Newman and Tami Knight.
            p.   cm.
ISBN 0-89732-207-X
1. Ropework. 2. Knots and splices.   I. Knight, Tami, 1959-.
    II. Title.
TT840.R66N48   1997
640'.41--dc21   97-4457
                                                       CIP

Printed in the United States of America
Published by Menasha Ridge Press
First edition, first printing

Illustrations by Tami Knight
Text design by Clay White
Cover design by Grant Tatum

Menasha Ridge Press
700 South 28th Street
Suite 206
Birmingham, Alabama 35233
(800) 247-9437

CONTENTS

Dedication

For the *greenies* on the mountain.

—Bob Newman

This is for you, mum.

—Tami Knight

Acknowledgments

Special thanks go to Mike Jones for the idea and the insight. And as always, to Susan and Britta.

—Bob Newman

Special thanks to all my friends at Menasha Ridge Press, my family, and the Phoenix Gymnastics team for helping me maintain my sanity.

—Tami Knight

KNOTS AROUND THE HOME

A Practical Guide for Practical People

Bob Newman and
Tami Knight

With illustrations
by Tami Knight

INTRODUCTION

Rope is confusing stuff. It's something that is always around but never noticed until it's needed. You can find it in drawers, in boxes, in the garage, in a pile in the corner, stuffed in the toolbox, hidden in the doghouse, lashed around a tree, even hanging from a branch. You'll rarely find it in a neat coil, bound, or still packaged. It's rarely kept in the garage, shed, or work shop, and it's rarely kept in good condition. Rope is an essential element of much household construction. It may not be holding your house together (or maybe it is), but it could be making it a safer and more enjoyable environment.

The reason rope is so confusing is because it's so versatile. We are constantly using rope to tie things up, tie things down, tie things together, and tie things apart. Rope is good for making things stay where you want them to. It is easy to use, but difficult to use well. As a nation, we are buying more homes and spending more time in them. As a consequence, our homes' utility and safety have become more important. The primary reason for writing this book has been to remind the ordinary person about the usefulness and practicality of rope while educating him/her about the safe use of it. Believe it or not, there is a special knot you can use for every situation that may arise in your home. This book is designed to show these situations, and teach you how to tie the right knot.

○ The gate was left open and Fido escaped. You know
   exactly where he's gone . . . to visit the poodle down the
   street. Rope can't keep the prima donna poodle from
   being in heat, but it can keep Fido from becoming the
   neighborhood stud. Grab a piece of rope from the trunk
   of your car and rush after Fido. When you find him, he's

1

halfway up the six-foot, chain-link fence, and you've got to act fast. Tying a knot in the rope to make a leash for the dog isn't as easy as it sounds. Can you use a "granny" knot? Grandma can't restrain Fido, the hormonal hound. That knot will slip before you can say "down boy!" You've got to come up with something better. . . .

○ Your teenage daughter is washing/drying one pair of jeans and a T-shirt three times a day. The electric company has threatened to put a lien on your salary unless you pay your overdue bill. Since you can't build your own hydro-electric dam in the backyard, you have two choices: send your daughter to work for the electric company or disconnect the dryer and tie a clothesline in the back yard.

○ You're growing a small garden in the yard, and it's beginning to look like "The Attack of the Killer Tomatoes." Your spouse tells you to build a trellis and tie up the vines. Don't use just any rope.

○ Your son is starting baseball practice, and you need to fit him, his three friends, 10 bats, a bucket of balls, 10 gloves, 15 helmets, two tee-ball stands, and the team's new uniforms into your Fiat. Can't close the trunk of the car? Need to tie it down? There's a fast, easy way with the proper knot.

○ Hurricane Bertha slam-dunked a fireplug through your sister's roof and you have to help her tie a tarp over the hole. If you want to be sure nothing else comes through the hole in her roof, you need to tie the tarp properly. Use a granny knot and she could be knee-deep in water by morning.

○ Your six-year-old won a life-size triceratops at the state fair. What? You'd rather drag it home with you than weather Junior's mother-of-all-tantrums? You'd better be sure Tommy the Triceratops stays on the roof of your car; there's no sense involving the police in a silly accident on the interstate. Believe it or not, there's a right and wrong rope for the job.

○ And what about when . . . well, you get the picture.

We all use ropes and knots around the house. In fact, you probably tie about four times as many knots as you might think. This little book is designed to help you select the right rope and then tie the right knot for any situation that might arise around your home. Because you can't teach Fido to control his hormonal urges, get the tomatoes to stand at attention, instruct Bertha where to inflict her fury, or satisfy Junior with a package of Sea Monkeys and cotton candy, it's easier for you to learn the ropes and tie the knots that other people use every day.

ROPE MAINTENANCE FOR DUMMIES

Rope is made from fibers whose origin is natural, synthetic, or a combination of the two. These fibers are either twisted or braided together into a continuous and uniform filament to make a rope.

When in its original, intact state, the rope has a property called *tensile strength*. This is the amount of force which, when applied to the rope, will cause it to break. The packaging in which rope comes will usually have the rope's tensile strength listed on it. Another specification that you might find on the packaging is the rope's *recommended work load*. This amount is often recorded in pounds and refers to the amount of weight that can be safely lifted or pulled with the rope. Any load beyond this figure could cause damage to the rope. Although the recommended work load is not relevant to every job, the tensile strength usually is. And if the tensile strength is known, the work load can be derived from it; it's usually about 10 percent of the tensile strength.

That's why using ropes you have around the house—the hunk of rope your dad gave you ten years ago, or the piece left by the previous tenant, or that old piece of climbing rope you bought from "Rubber Spine" Rob—is a bit precarious. Using used rope is like driving a used car; you never know what happened to it before it came into your possession. Any kind of undue stress makes rope weaker and more susceptible to breaks.

Mountaineers, sailors, kayakers, rock climbers, spelunkers, and rescue personnel use ropes extensively, sometimes in life-and-death situations. Because their lives depend on the careful use and maintenance of ropes, they *never* use borrowed or secondhand ropes.

And though you may not be using a rope to climb the side of your house or ride the rapids in your backyard, it's important to remember that a broken rope can spell disaster even in a casual situation.

Remember Junior's giant triceratops? You're zippin' along the interstate; Junior is wreathed in smiles; and Tommy the Triceratops is tied to the roof of the car (sort of). Sure the rope smelled a bit like gasoline, and you were a little surprised to find it in your trunk (since you couldn't remember putting it there), but you tied plenty of knots and the dinosaur didn't move much when you pulled it. What could go wrong?

Well, you'd better hope your insurance company covers flying triceratops because Tommy just took a nose dive through the windshield of the car behind you. And you'd better believe a head-on collision with a dinosaur at 60 mph can do some serious damage. Did I hear that guy say something about his lawyer?

○ The Big Four

There are four nasty factors which, on their own or in combination with one another, can weaken your rope whether in storage or in use. Friction, overtension, corrosive substances, and dirt can all render your rope as useless as a lump of wet spaghetti.

Friction

Friction damage can occur when a rope rubs against itself or another rope in a nonbinding manner (binding, or course, means "tied by knots"). Friction damage can also happen when a rope rubs against another object, such as a rock, a tree branch, or a fence post. Friction of either type can be extremely debilitating to a rope, and in some cases can cause a rope to snap very quickly and unexpectedly. The heat that friction produces can melt synthetic fiber ropes and sometimes burn natural fiber ropes. Rubbing against a hard or sharp surface in conjunction with heat can also cut and tear a natural rope. Heat can damage a rope within seconds, and there is no formula to predict when a certain rope will break or become damaged by friction. Whether a rope becomes damaged or breaks depends on the material of the rope—cotton, polyethylene, nylon—the amount of surface-to-surface contact, the speed at which the two surfaces are being rubbed against each other, and the pressure being applied to the ropes in opposite directions. Of course, the best way to prevent damage is to minimize friction. If you are running a rope in any situation over a sharp edge—like the edge of your roof—use an old towel or a rope sleeve (available in climbing catalogs) between the rope and the sharp edge.

If your ropes have already been exposed to possible friction, it's relatively easy to distinguish friction burns on most ropes. A contrasting shine along a section of the rope which often has a smoother feel to the touch than the rest of the rope indicates a slight burn. Some ropes will show fibers which appear almost melted.

If a rope has friction burns you should be very careful not to overload it, and never use friction-burned rope for any critical purpose, such as towing a car or hoisting something heavy. If you know a rope has severe friction damage, throw it away.

Overtension

When a light rope is used for a heavy job or when a rope is shock loaded (that is, loaded too quickly), the rope can sustain damage from overtension. Overtension damage is very much like straining a muscle. A fibrous rope can be damaged much like a fibrous muscle; trying to lift something too fast that's too heavy can cause the fibers to become weak or torn. Depending on the material and the method used to construct the rope, overtension can weaken a rope internally in varying degrees. You should always use a rope in compliance with the recommended work load.

Because of the nature of this type of damage, inspection of ropes is somewhat problematic. Identifying internal weaknesses is not as easy as finding external damage. Some ropes can be "opened" by twisting the fibers in the opposite direction from which they lie. Inspecting a rope this way, section by section, you can sometimes spot torn or frayed fiber. Since you can't always take a rope apart without destroying it, however, internal fibers that are damaged often go unnoticed. Furthermore, overtension is often manifested in stretched fibers, not torn ones. And, just like the muscles in our bodies, a stretched rope, even though it's not torn, is still much weaker than a healthy one, and prone to more tears.

To avoid damaging your rope by overtension, ensure that your rope's recommended work load is adequate for the job at hand. And take care to load the rope slowly and smoothly, just as if you were lifting, pulling, pushing, or holding the load with your own muscles. If you don't know the tensile strength or the recommended work load, use common sense and recognize that even a strong-looking rope might easily break. Remember, too, that different ropes have different stretching properties; what is safe for one might be dangerous for another.

Corrosive Substances

To provide a list of all substances that can cause damage to a rope is simply unrealistic. Acid or other caustic substances, oil, gas, mildew, and sunlight are just a few examples of agents that can damage your rope.

Inspection of ropes for corrosive damage is fairly simple. Often, the damage can be estimated from a rope's obvious exposure to corrosive elements. If a rope is stored outside or used for a tire swing or clothesline, it is safe to assume that the rope has gradually weakened over time. From the natural effects of weather alone (rain, sunlight, wind, etc.) most ropes lose 30 percent of their strength in two years of continual exposure. Or, if a rope has been stored against or near a gas container, the chances are high that the rope has sustained some corrosive damage from the gasoline fumes. But if you're not sure about the kind or amount of exposure, a rope can be inspected. Using the same technique for examining a rope internally for tension damage, untwist the cords of the rope and look for stains or discoloration: corrosives often leave a stain in the fibers of the rope. You may also be able to smell the substance's residue still lingering on the fibers of the rope. Treat any section of rope that might have been damaged by corrosives as having been weakened; cut the affected section from the length of the rope and use the two shorter pieces separately or tie them together with a fisherman's knot.

Unfortunately, cleaning does nothing to restore a rope damaged by corrosives. Careful use and proper storage, however, will ensure that your rope doesn't come in contact with them. Store your rope neatly coiled, in a dry and well-ventilated place. Ideally, this place should be cool and not receive any direct sunlight. Never store a rope outside—Mother Nature will ruin it for you. Ropes that have been soaked in salt water ought to be rinsed in fresh water and air dried thoroughly in the shade before being stored away.

Ropes left in-situ, like a clothesline or tire swing, need to be inspected regularly to check for damage from outdoor elements. In the case of the swing, should any damage be evident, the rope *must* be replaced. Buying another rope will be much cheaper than the insurance deductible for Junior's emergency room visit.

Dirt

Some of the worst offenders when it comes to causing covert damage to ropes are sand and dirt. These perfidious little particles burrow themselves between the fibers of ropes, and the movement involved in using the ropes causes the tiny particles to rub against the fibers. This action slowly but surely weakens and eventually destroys the rope.

Beware of the dirty, gritty rope! Storage, proper use, and cleaning of a rope are critical if you intend to use it for a long time. Remember, you can wash a rope in your washing machine on the gentle cycle with Woolite. A soft scrub brush and soft soap like Dove can be used to clean a rope, but don't use bleach or other solvents—they are corrosives. Remember, a clean rope is a happy rope.

○ Inspection of Suspect Ropes

Careful inspection of ropes can reveal damage. It is wise to inspect rope both before and after use. Ropes can be damaged by improper use and storage, exposure to the elements, and more improbable factors like Fido, the munching machine.

To inspect your rope, uncoil it and feel it along the entire length. Look for broken fibers, melted fibers, stains, discoloration, rot, mildew, and just plain ol' dirt. Upon careful inspection, any immediate weakness can be discovered by sight. If any one of the defects mentioned above is present, your rope may be weakened.

If you find or suspect your rope has been damaged, there are several things you can do before discarding it. Though you can't know the extent of the damage just by seeing it, you should assume the worst; any sign of weakness should be eradicated. Damaged rope can be salvaged for lightweight jobs if the damage is extensive

or troublesome to repair. You can cut the rope, throw out the damaged portion and retie the rope with a fisherman's knot; or you can cut the rope, throw out the damaged part, and use the shortened pieces for jobs that can use shorter ropes. If you cannot cut the rope, you can tie a shortening knot and thus bypass the damage. Ropes that are merely tangled can usually be untwisted gently. And, of course, you may need to wash your rope. You should put your washing machine on its delicate cycle, use a soft scrub brush on persistent stains, and use a soap for fine washables, such as Woolite or Ivory Snow—never detergents or solvents. Air dry the rope in a shady place, out of reach of Fido (who may still be miffed at you for wrecking his evening with Fifi). And in any case, it is necessary to bear in mind that any rope that has been damaged will now be weaker, no matter how well you clean or repair it.

○ Whipping the Rope

Whipping a rope is quite different from whipping a person. (We'll cover the *uses* of rope in another chapter. . . .) *Whipping a rope* refers to sealing the ends so they do not fray. It can be done by applying a thin but strong length of cord neatly around the rope's end.

Lay the whipping cord in a loop just below the end of the rope. Starting at the bottom of the loop, wrap the whipping back over the loop lying along the rope. Keeping the coils tight and right up against each other, continue until the coils you are forming are as long as the rope is wide. Pinch the whipping tightly against the rope to prevent the coils from unwrapping and pass it through the loop. Pull the running end of the whipping tight (away from the end of the rope) to make the remainder of the loop disappear.

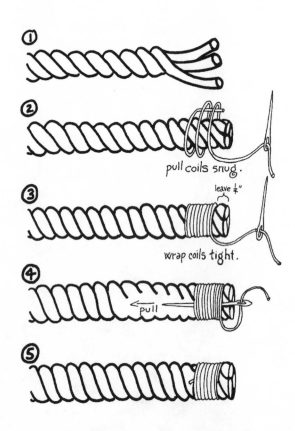

①

② pull coils snug.

③ leave ¼"

wrap coils tight.

④ ←pull

⑤

An easier way to whip a rope is to use electrician's tape. Specialty climbing stores offer a similar tape that's more expensive but comes in an array of exciting colors. But simple, black, electrician's tape works just fine.

Just wrap a piece around the end of the rope tightly a couple of turns, maybe three. Keep the coils flat—no ridges or bumps.

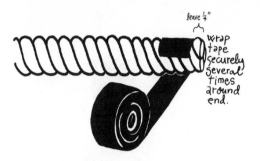

Many ropes can be whipped by burning the ends. Depending on the material, the reaction to flame is quite spectacular. Synthetic ropes can be heat sealed because their fibers melt. They do not produce a flame, but the melted synthetic material can still produce a nasty burn, so be careful. Natural fiber ropes do produce a flame, but do not melt. Thus, it is ineffective to whip a natural fiber rope by flame; however, burning the end of a natural hemp rope in a crowd often produces outstanding reactions on the faces of nearby people.

Apply the flame of a lighter directly to the end of the rope. In a few seconds the rope will start to burn and melting nylon will likely drip. Let it burn and seal itself; when you can't see the individual fibers amid the flames, the rope is sealed. Put out the flame but remember that the end of the rope where it is now sealed is still hot and will remain so for a few seconds.

○ Coiling the Rope

Ropes should always be coiled before being stored away. A coiled rope is more easily kept out of the way and is less likely to become damaged.

To begin you need to form your rope into a neat pile of coils. You can effectively do this two ways:

Coil the rope by winding it loosely around the palm/elbow. . . .

Coil the rope by making loops in one hand and holding them in the other.

14

After the coils of the rope are gathered together, leave one end free and use it to snug the coils together as follows:

Wrap the end around the coils three or four times.

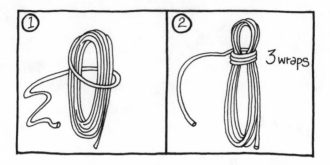

Make a loop in the rope and run it through the upper coils.

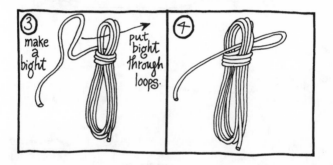

Pull the loop open and bend it over the top of the loops.

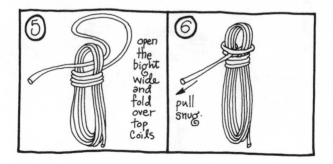

Pull the end of the rope and snug it all together.

LEARNING THE ROPES: THE ARRAY OF AVAILABLE FIBERS

Before the getting into the specifics of tying knots, it's a good idea to get a handle on the definition of "rope." You've probably heard rope called a number of things: cord, cordage, line, twine, string, etc. A sailor will call a rope a rope when it's *not* used around water, but it's a "line" when used around water. String, twine, and cordage are different, too. But to keep things simple, anything used to tie a knot in this book will be referred to as rope.

That doesn't mean all ropes are the same, however. Unlike the rose (a rose is a rose is a rose), a rope isn't always just a rope. The right rope is needed for every job. The wrong rope could get you in a mess of trouble. For instance, use the wrong rope to tie Fido in the yard, and Fifi, the poodle next door, might end up with a litter of adorable, black-and-brown, spotted poodle-hounds. So that you can differentiate, what follows is the array of available fibers.

Natural Fibers

For the most part, synthetic ropes have replaced natural fibers. Natural fiber ropes weaken easily when "shocked" (overloaded suddenly). And, although they are resistant to ultraviolet light, they tend to rot and grow mildew. They require more care than synthetics, and do not handle as nicely. And, of course, the synthetic ropes are available in an assortment of bright, beautiful colors. However, natural fiber ropes are cheap, and for lightweight house, garden, craft, and picnic duty, they are perfectly adequate.

Coir

Only good for light use and backyard luau drinks, coir is made from coconut fibers. It lasts only a short while, stretches like mad, and is very susceptible to the elements. Good luck finding it in your local hardware store!

Cotton

Cotton rope comes either twisted or braided. It's an inexpensive and relatively attractive rope, but it's not very strong. Cotton rope is soft and handles nicely, and it holds knots very well; in fact, if the rope becomes wet, it's almost impossible to break a knot. Though it may not be ideal for the sailboat or canoe, cotton rope is excellent for three-legged races, tying a picnic tarp, and other light household jobs.

What about those pesky tomatoes? Because it rots, cotton rope is good for tying up plants. At the end of the season, both the plant and the rope can be tossed into the compost.

And Junior's carnival prize? Of all ropes, cotton is the *least* resistant to friction, overtension, corrosive substances, and cutting/tearing. So, *don't* tie Tommy the Triceratops to the roof of the Toyota with a cotton rope.

Jute and Sisal

Jute is a thin, twisted rope best suited for macramé, lightweight chores, and tying up small objects like Uncle Fred's birthday present (if he'd been a little nicer last Christmas, he might've gotten a ribbon and priority mailing instead).

Sisal is much tougher than jute and also made into twisted ropes. For the light- to medium-weight jobs, it's a better choice. It's more decorative than packing tape for tying up boxes of seasonal decorations or old tax records.

Flax

Flax is the coarse material used to make refined linen, so you can imagine how tough it is. It's mostly used to make small diameter cord. It also makes a great twine for simple or decorative tasks.

Hemp

Hemp has been used in Asia for centuries and is currently popular there, but it's been replaced by synthetics in North America. Despite the efforts of Grateful Dead types and organic gardeners, it has been banished from the rope scene in many countries because of its association with the drug, marijuana. Until recently though, hemp was the best material available for ropes. Despite its waning popularity, hemp handles well and stands up nicely to natural elements.

○ Synthetic Fibers

As the name implies, synthetic ropes are made of man-made materials. Chemists have done more than promote fashion faux pas like coke-bottle glasses, white lab coats, tube socks with loafers, and pocket protectors. They've synthesized long chains of molecules into wonder fibers like polypropylene, polyester, polyamide (nylon), and the aramid fibers (Kevlar). Like many things scientists have developed, synthetics are often better than their natural counterparts.

Polypropylene

Polypropylene ropes can be twisted or braided and are available in a variety of sizes from thin string to one-inch-diameter rope. They are the cheapest of the synthetics but are not particularly resistant to abrasion or ultraviolet light. In fact, they can be damaged by heat in excess of only 150 degrees Fahrenheit. They are, however, resistant to rot, mildew, and other corrosive subtances.

This makes them excellent all-purpose ropes. You can use them for anything around the house or yard, but they should be inspected often if used regularly at their recommended work load or left in-situ for extended periods of time. Case in point: if the guy next door is a former Marine who knows how to do the Mongolian Neck Twist, either keep his kid away from your tire swing or check that rope once a month. Otherwise, the kid won't be the only one with a stiff neck and missing teeth.

Nylon

Nylon is more expensive than polypropylene, but it's a better product. Whether twisted or braided, it's resistant to *all* factors that damage ropes and it holds knots well. From thin strings for handyman jobs and crafts to high-tech climbing ropes, nylon is strong, resilient, and versatile.

Use nylon to tie the tarp over the hole in your sister's roof or to secure the triceratops to the top of the Toyota. But remember to avoid those low overpasses on the way home; nylon isn't indestructible, and you could find yourself the next entry on the web at http://www.news of the terribly odd.com.

Polyester

It's not just for powder-blue leisure suits anymore! Polyester ropes handle well and are resistant to factors that damage most ropes. They are just as effective as nylon ropes but stretch less. This makes them great for dog leashes and running lines, clotheslines, and hauling the lawnmower out of the neighbor's swimming pool. (Maybe Junior should wait a few years before shouldering yard chores.) But keep in mind, if you use polyester rope around water, it won't float, so keep a hand on it.

Aramids

If you're a Rambo-type, and you've got a pile of money, aramid fibers are just your style! You can truthfully tell your neighbors that your prizewinning pit bull is tied up with rope stronger than steel. Although Killer, the four-legged set of teeth, can probably gnaw through it, he won't be able to snap it.

Kevlar, Dyneema, and *Spectra* are the trademarks for these expensive specialty ropes. They are used by the military, outdoor activity extremists, and the attendant rescue personnel. For knots around the house, however, aramid fiber ropes are more than you'll need.

Polyethylene

Polyethylene fibers produce a rope of undesirable characteristics. Unless you really want your sister's rooftop tarp to come loose during a rainstorm, you should use a rope made from nylon, polyester, or polypropylene.

KNOT THE ROPES!

For as long as human beings have had conscious thought patterns, they've probably used knots for utilitarian and decorative purposes. Over centuries of use, certain knots have been designed, perfected, and tailored for very specific tasks. Many knots are designed to tie easily in many different kinds of rope, some are designed to cinch upon themselves to prevent slipping, some are designed to untie more readily than others, and others are designed to remain intact forever.

Sure, you can *get by* using the "granny knot" for all purposes. However, learning to tie the proper knot for every situation will lessen your frustration and the likelihood of having an accident. A lawyer may not know the difference between a hitch and a figure 8, but he will know the difference between Tommy the Triceratops on the roof of your Toyota and Tommy in the front seat of his client's new Mercedes (about $1,500, plus lawyer fees).

Twenty thousand years ago, Og and Ug used a bowline knot to tie the rope around the woolly mammoth and tow it back to the fire ring. Today, you can use that very same knot to hang your hammock.

Rope Parts Defined

A. *Bitter End (a.k.a. Standing End):* the other end of the rope.

B. *Standing Part:* the rope between the running and bitter ends.

C. *Bight:* a loop which doesn't cross over itself.

D. *Running End:* the end you are working with (the lead).

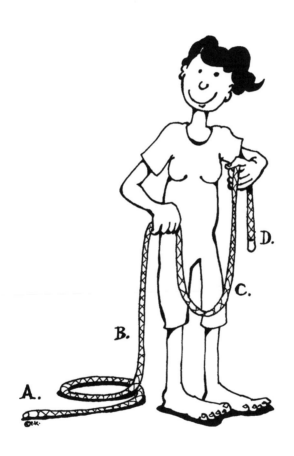

○ Knot Parts Defined

A Loop

Loops form the beginning of many knots. A loop can be made underhand or overhand. An underhand loop is formed by the running end crossing beneath the standing part. An overhand loop is formed by the running end crossing over the standing part.

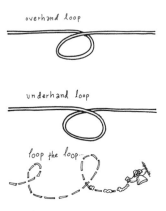

A Turn or a Round Turn

A turn has the rope run around an object, like a fence post or tree, one complete time. When the rope has gone around twice, you have a round turn.

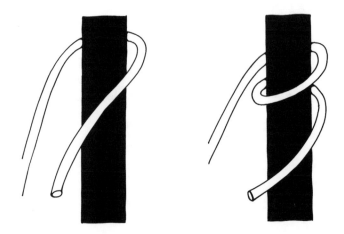

A Tuck

A tuck is formed by making the running end into a small bight. When a tuck is used as the lead and inserted back into a knot, it makes a "quick release," or a slipknot. You can disassemble the knot by pulling on the running end of your rope; the tuck is easily slipped back through the insertion point of the knot.

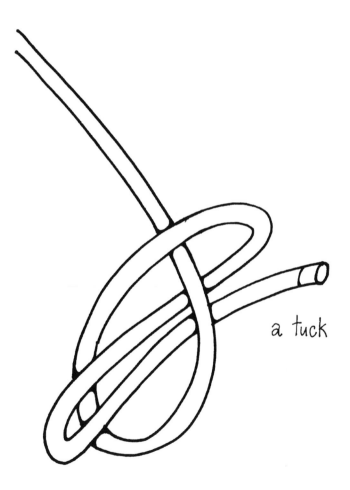

a tuck

○ The Bowline Knot

Without question, this is the most important knot you'll ever learn. The bowline is easy to tie in most ropes, will not slip, and is easy to undo even after hours of tension. Set and dressed, your bowline will have a distinctive look.

And here is the best method of tying a bowline.

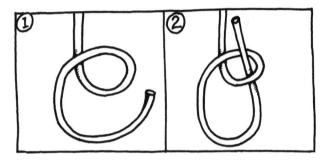

Make an overhand loop. Then, holding the loop in one hand, pass the running end through the loop from below.

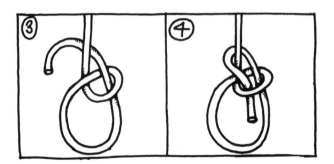

Pass the running end behind the standing part above the loop. Now bring it around and pass back through the overhand loop.

Pull snug by the running end.

It is also possible to tie a bowline into a rope while it is under tension.

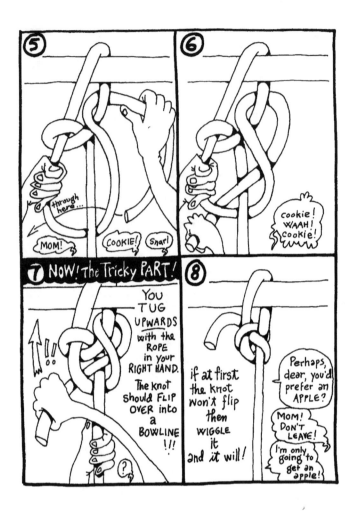

○ Stopping Knots

Two simple knots which can be used to weight one end of a rope or stop it from pulling through an aperture are the overhand knot and the figure 8 knot.

The Overhand

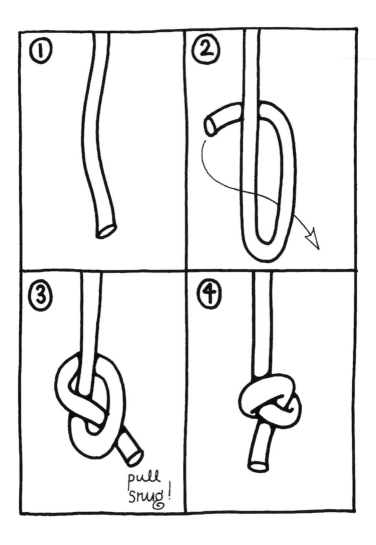

The Figure 8

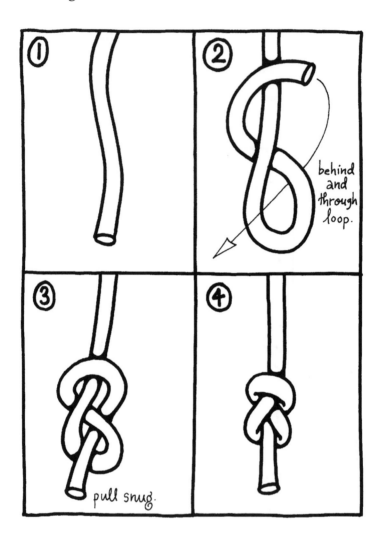

② behind and through loop.

③ pull snug.

○ Hitches

A hitch is used to tie a rope to an object. Hitches are quick and easy to tie.

Half Hitch

The half hitch is not a secure knot by itself, but, used in conjunction with a round turn or a trucker's hitch, it becomes useful and sturdy.

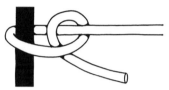

Clove Hitch

The clove hitch is an excellent knot which binds unto itself. It is much easier to adjust than the bowline knot. A clove hitch can be tied two ways:

> Pass the running end around the object counterclockwise. Now, make a second turn above the first.

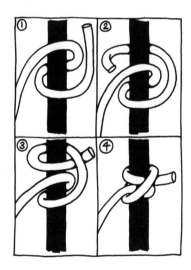

Now, put the running end through that loop. (To make a slipped clove hitch, tuck the running end back through the knot.) Pull snug.

This method works if you can drop the loops of the clove hitch around the object:

Form an overhand loop and an underhand loopnext to one another.

Place the underhand loop beneath the overhand loop to form one opening.

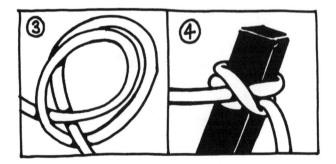

Drop the two loops over the object and snug the loops together.

The Trucker's Hitch

This hitch is actually a system of knots that gives you a mechanical advantage for taking up slack. Thus, it is wonderful for securing things to your car. Tie down that triceratops with a trucker's hitch!

Since this knot is cranked tight, you should always use synthetic rope of an appropriate size.

And here's the best method for tying a trucker's hitch:

> Tie a quick release loop (see page 27) above the tie-down point. Pass the running end around the tie-down point, then pass the running end through the quick release loop.
>
> Pull down on the running end. Haul on it. Take in the slack.

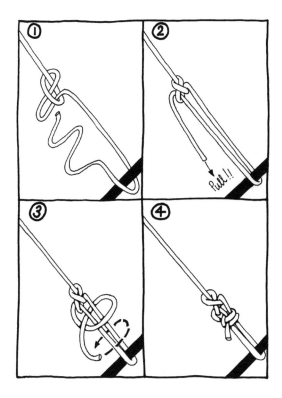

> Pinch the running end around the standing part below the quick release.
>
> Secure it with two or three half hitches.

○ Joining Knots (Tying One Rope to Another)

Knots which join one rope to another are the most commonly used knots. If you have a damaged rope that has been cut into good parts, or if the rope you have is too short and you need to tie another one to it, there are two safe knots available to you: the sheet bend and the fisherman's knot.

The Sheet Bend

The sheet bend is an excellent knot that binds well and can be used for two ropes of different types or sizes. To tie the sheetbend, form a bight with the thicker of the ropes. Push the running end of the thinner rope up through the bight and underneath both parts of the bight, then push it under the standing part of itself without going back down through the bight.

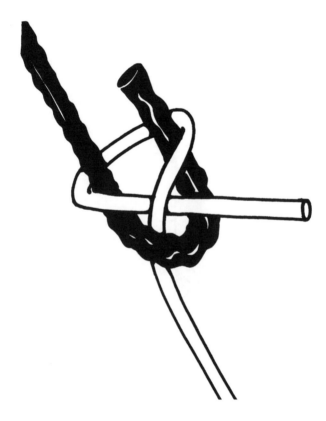

The Fisherman's Knot

This knot, once set, can become difficult to undo. But when attaching two ropes, this quality is usually desirable! This is a strong and excellent knot, and it's ridiculously simple. Make an overhand knot and leave it open. Pass the running end of the other rope through it and make an overhand knot with that running end around the other rope.

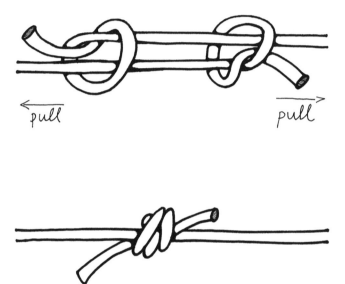

○ The Square Knot

A simple knot to tie a bandage, the laundry bag, a garbage bag, a bandanna, or the legs of a turkey. One of the most common misuses of this knot is tying it to attach two ropes together. Never use it for this purpose because the square knot has a tendency to invert or "capsize." This means that when tension is applied to the rope, the knot will flip over and slip apart.

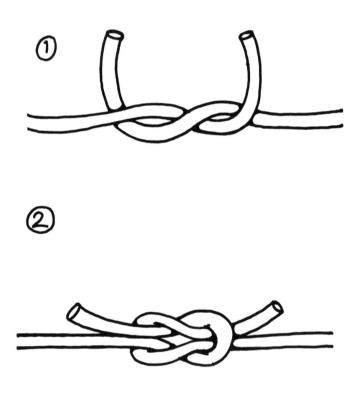

○ Shortening Knots

If you don't have a knife (or a pet beaver) handy to cut away a damaged portion of rope, or if you simply need to temporarily shorten a rope, you can tie a knot in the rope to bypass any section of it.

Make a bight of rope ensuring that all parts that have been damaged are well within the bight. Tie an overhand knot at the base of the bight. Take note that no shortening knot will make the rope as strong as it was before the damage occurred. The knot will help, but the rope's original strength has been compromised. Caveat!

Sheepshank

More complex than the simple overhand knot but with one advantage: if the rope is ever put under tension, the force pulls *through* the knot rather than against it.

Also, women take note: not a lot of guys know of or have even heard of this knot. Could amount to a cachet if you're in the singles market. Just start out by saying "It's a *sheepshank* knot. *Funny* you've *never* heard of it. Want me to show it to you?" You can take it from there.

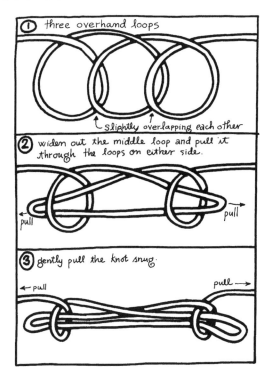

○ Knots for Fun

Now that you're confident with the more utilitarian knots, here are two that are lots of fun at parties or at home.

The Dragon Bowline

After telling the other guests about your knot-tying ability, build the suspense about your self-designed, fully patented knot, the Dragon Bowline. Whip together a simple bowline, hold the standing end in one hand, toss the knot to the floor, and wait for a drumroll. Walk away pulling the knot behind you. When you see the quizzical looks, tell them you're "dragon" the bowline. It's hysterical.

The Comeback Knot

This trick demands an air of sexual pique or humor and a naïve but curious person. After selecting the victim, tie him/her up and leave the room (or the house). When the victim realizes you're not going to return, he or she should begin to yell "Come back! Come back!" (among other things). This is loads of fun, too.

USING THE ROPES!

○ The Bowline Knot

Here are some examples of situations where the bowline knot would be the safe way to go.

Simple rope swing   Use a thick diameter synthetic rope. Remember to inspect the rope regularly for damage.

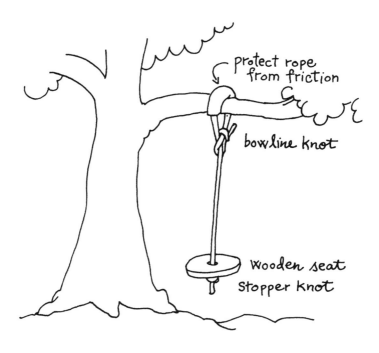

protect rope
from friction

bowline knot

wooden seat
stopper knot

Tying up a hammock Use a 3/8″ or heavier synthetic rope. If the neighborhood kids are prone to impromptu "dogpiles" in the hammock, you may want to use a rope with a recommended work load greater than 500 lb!

Leash Depending on Fido's weight class (flyweight, welterweight, or "is that thing a dog or a horse?" weight), the recommended work load for this rope may be as little as 50 lb. or as great as 150 lb.

Tying a small picnic tarp   Use a synthetic rope if the tarp will be semi-permanent; a natural rope is sufficient for day use. Remember, polyester is the least stretchable of all rope material and withstands the natural elements well. Be sure to consider the weight of rainwater if the tarp is used in foul weather.

Tying a dog run   A good synthetic rope is perfect for this job since it can withstand the friction and tension of Fido's Movement, as well as the natural elements. Stay away from natural fiber ropes like cotton.

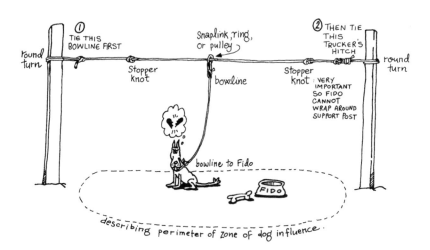

43

Tying a tire swing   A synthetic rope is a good choice for this task. Because it stretches less than other synthetics, a polyester rope is perfect.

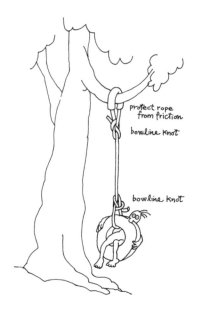

protect rope
from friction

bowline knot

bowline knot

Pulling a sled or wagon   You can use almost any rope for this job. Be sure, however, that the rope is not damaged. Breaking a rope while pulling four kids on a sled could hurl you down the hill on your face!

bowline

44

Tying a boat to a cleat (or ring) Use a polypropylene rope of appropriate diameter depending on the size and weight of your boat.

bowline
to the
" Guppy "

Guppy

clove hitch
around post

...or bowline knot
to wharf

○ Stopping Knots

Two simple knots which can be used to weight one end of a rope or stop it from pulling through an aperture are the overhand knot and the figure 8 knot.

Here is how these knots may be used.

protect rope over tree branch

bowline knot

figure·8 stopper knot

figure·8 stopper knots

○ Hitches

Clove Hitch

Here are some odd jobs where you'll find a clove hitch comes in handy.

Tying a rope to a tarp without grommets   If you are using a big sheet of borrowed plastic as a tarp, it's quite possible there will be no holes for attaching your rope. Since your brother threatened death if you destroyed his tarp, you can't just make your own holes. But you can attach the rope to the tarp without damaging it. Put a golf ball or a golf ball-sized rock behind the tarp where you want to attach the rope. Gather the tarp around the object making a pocket around it; it should look something like the wrapper of a lollipop. Use a strong but small-diameter natural or synthetic rope. Slip a clove hitch over the ball and secure around the plastic neck; attach the other end as needed to erect the tarp. Voilà! Your brother will never know.

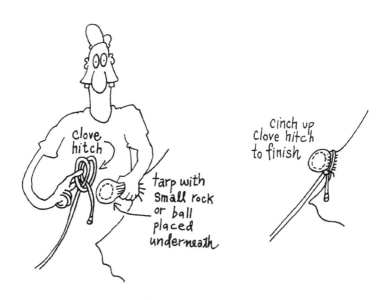

Tying a large tarp over something   Much of this will depend on the size of the tarp (handkerchief or football field) and the thing you're tying it over (Fido's doghouse or Yankee Stadium). If you need to nail the tarp down, put a strip of lathe over the tarp. Then the heads of the nails will not pull through the tarp. Here are several illustrated possibilities. Your situation may require a combination of these. Always use rope of appropriate size for the force that will be exerted upon it.

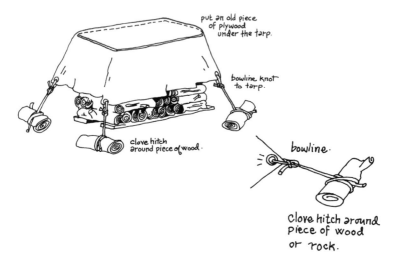

put an old piece of plywood under the tarp.

bowline knot to tarp.

clove hitch around piece of wood.

bowline.

Clove hitch around piece of wood or rock.

Tying Fido, a boat, or the neighbor's kid to a post   If Fido is aging gracefully, use a lightweight rope. If Fido is raging through canine puberty, you may want to consider a steel cable.

Clove hitch over post

The Trucker's Hitch

Here are some situations where the trucker's hitch will keep the lawyers at bay.

Lashing a load to a trailer or pick up truck   If you're traveling a long distance, it is wise to periodically check your rope and knots for damage from friction, tearing/cutting, and stretching. You may need to snug up the system along the way.

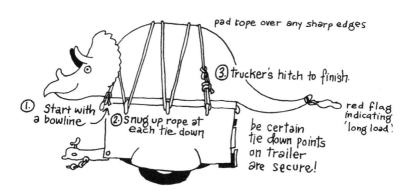

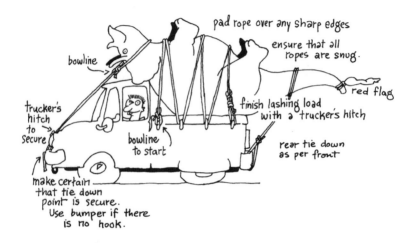

pad rope over any sharp edges

ensure that all ropes are snug.

bowline

red flag

trucker's hitch to Secure

finish lashing load with a trucker's hitch

bowline to start

rear tie down as per front

make certain that tie down point is secure. Use bumper if there is no hook.

Tying down the trunk of your car   If an object fits into the trunk of your car but the lid won't close, all you need is a length of rope about 1/4" in diameter. Find secure tie-down points on the lid of the trunk, as well as the body of the car. Be sure not to use open-ended secure points such as hooks since the knots can slip off them.

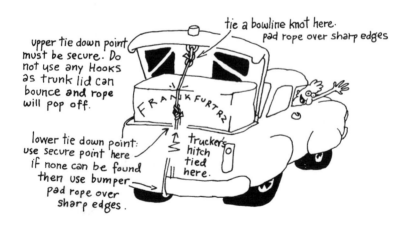

tie a bowline knot here.
pad rope over sharp edges

upper tie down point must be secure. Do not use any Hooks as trunk lid can bounce and rope will pop off.

FRANKFURTR

lower tie down point: use secure point here if none can be found then use bumper pad rope over sharp edges.

trucker's hitch tied here.

50

Tying down a big tarp   If you are tying down a really large tarp or circus tent, the mechanical advantage you get when you use the trucker's hitch will help make the thing more taut.

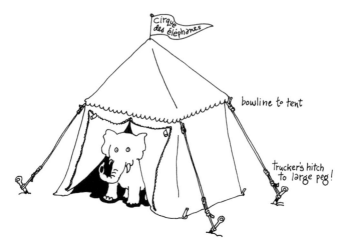

Tying down Tommy the Triceratops   When tying anything to the roof of your car, be sure to find secure points. Once again, don't use any open-ended secure points since knots can easily slide off them. Any object tied to a car is safest when tied to a secure roof rack; using your muffler as a tie-down point is not effective or safe. However, many automobiles are equipped with appropriate points on which to secure your ropes. Just be sure that every point you tie to, or loop through, is secure. Your system will only be as strong as the its weakest point.

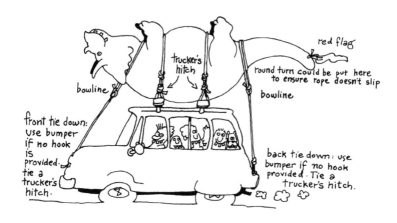

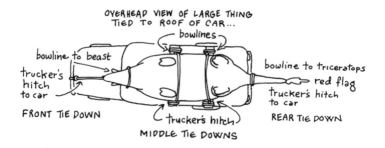

OVERHEAD VIEW OF LARGE THING
TIED TO ROOF OF CAR...

bowlines

bowline to beast

trucker's hitch to car

FRONT TIE DOWN

trucker's hitch

MIDDLE TIE DOWNS

bowline to triceratops

red flag

trucker's hitch to car

REAR TIE DOWN

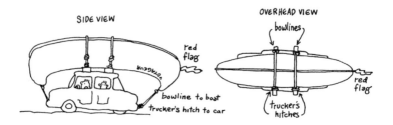

SIDE VIEW

red flag

VOYAGEUR

bowline to boat

trucker's hitch to car

OVERHEAD VIEW

bowlines

red flag

trucker's hitches

○ Shortening Knots

If you're still confused about the sheepshank, here's how to shorten a rope quickly and painlessly.

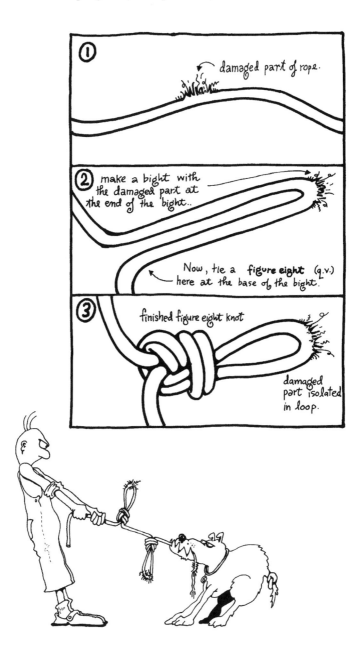